DRAMA DETOX

Stop Self-Sabotage

Before It Stops You

BY

DAUNE THOMPSON

Published by Create Space Publishing

ISBN-13: 978-1461065395
ISBN-10: 1461065399

idi coaching does not dispense medical advice or prescribe the use of any technique as a form of treatment for physical or medical problems without the advice of a physician,either directly or indirectly. The intent of idi coaching/training is only to offer information of a general nature to help you in your quest for emotional and spiritual well-being. In the event you use idi coaching principles for yourself, the owners of idi coaching (Open Mind Consulting) assume no responsibility for your actions.

Edited by Write Advisors
www.writeadvisors.com, Atlanta, GA

Designed by Lance Jaze
Scottsdale, AZ

DEDICATED TO MY GIRLS,
MY WAW

Also by Daune Thompson

∞

I Deserve It Dream Book
Kids Only

I Deserve It Dream Book
Adults Edition

I Deserve It
Motivational Training & Coaching

I Deserve It Products
*Inspirational jewelry, apparel,
and keychains*

For information about bulk purchases of this book
or other **idi** motivational materials,
please contact Daune Thompson at:

www.ideserveitnow.com
www.daunethompson.com
info@ideserveitnow.com

Forward

If you are serious about taking total control of your life and your future, Daune Thompson's new book, *Drama Detox*, is a must read.

Have you heard the concept that you know the right answers in your life but you continually make the wrong decisions? After you read this book, you will understand how to empower your decision-making process to win in the Present Moment and beyond.

Daune's personal journey to find success and happiness is shared in a way to give insight on how to deal with life's biggest challenges and breakthrough to live your greatest you. I coach and work with some of the most successful people on the planet and I will be sharing this book with everyone I know.

It's "reasons or results" in life and business: If you are interested in better results, this would be an excellent time to pick up your copy of *Drama Detox* today!

Bill Walsh

Venture Capitalist/Business Coach
www.billwalsh360.com

Introduction

When's the last time you heard something like this:

- "There was so much DRAMA, I just couldn't take it!"
- "He's dating a DRAMA Queen."
- "There's DRAMA going on at work."

If you're like most people, you've probably heard the word "drama" pretty recently. When you say *drama*, it almost prepares your listener for what kind of conversation is about to unfold. The examples are everywhere, but the solution is quite simple: DETOX!

As I began writing this book, I realized drama is primarily what we watch happening outside of ourselves. We let it affect us, discouraging us from getting what we deserve. Drama can be the main force working against our goals and accomplishments. Most personal challenges that confront us originate with the drama of work, friends, partners, kids, relationships, social groups and family that we allow to get out of control. That's when we begin to lose our grip on doing what we want in life. We make the wrong decisions and we follow the wrong paths. Thus, we create even more drama because we are now on a path that makes us unhappy.

If you have ever overindulged in anything in your life, you know how crappy you feel afterwards: You know, like eating an entire fudge sundae with three scoops at one sitting. You want to just purge it. Usually, you suffer through it until enough time passes and you feel better.

The body that goes through food, drug, alcohol, emotional, chemical, or any type of overindulgence or intoxication needs to detox. As painful as physical detoxing can be, it's worth it to feel cleaner, freer and "lighter," you might say.

Like the body, the mind also needs time and a good cleanse to begin working properly after being "under the drama influence." The same goes for mental detoxing. We can detox the drama from our lives so we don't feel so crappy any more. Drama tends to weigh on us emotionally. Then, it begins to affect other areas of our lives, which can lead to physical or psychological symptoms. We can make ourselves sick and our lives unfulfilling if we don't rid ourselves from the cause. In essence, we self-sabotage.

My intention for this book is to give you both the knowledge to be aware of self-sabotage and the tools to intercept the drama. This book is written not to motivate you like a cheerleading squad with pompoms; it is written to awaken you to the power you have *inside*.

You are a gift to everyone you meet in some way. It is my hope that you find the power within yourself to let others be touched by your magnificent gifts. Detoxing from the drama in your life allows you to more freely express your gifts and pursue your goals.

This book, *Drama Detox*, is the latest publication from my companies, **idi – I Deserve It** and **Open Mind Consulting.** We are dedicated inspiring people to overcome their challenges and fears, to lead them to create a more effective and successful business or personal life. In the last part of *Drama Detox*, we explain the **idi** system so that you can practice the detox training in context of the whole offering.

If you have questions or want more information, email **idi** at **info@ideserveitnow. com**. Feel free to share what you've experienced with us to help others as well. We look forward to hearing from you.

Wishing you the life you truly Deserve,

Daune

How to Use This Book

As young children, we were often told not to write in our books. You've heard it: "Don't get it dirty. Keep it clean." This is a little different.

This is *your* book. Get it dirty. Write all over it. Use the Journal Spot in the back to put down in your own words what you want to remember and incorporate into your life. I encourage you to underline the areas that make you wonder. Write out questions that come up. Draw pictures to get you thinking of possibilities.

You may also want to put special attention into answering or addressing the I Deserve It (**idi**) tips provided at the end of each chapter. They'll help you get thinking in the right direction.

But most of all, enjoy the journey.

CONTENTS

PART I:
WELCOME TO
DRAMA DETOX

1

THE DRAMA STEW

Every person, all the events of your life are there because
you have drawn them there. What you choose to do with
them is up to you. -Richard Bach

Drama – That word is so descriptive. Someone says it
and you know immediately what's going on. Admit it, we
all love it. It's easy to spot, it's easy to create, and it's
safe. Drama – safe? Yes, that's what I said, safe. For a
long time, I struggled to understand the reason why so
many of us are staying in the same place doing the same
things while expecting different results. The answer is
this: We are comfortable when doing things the same
way, even if it results in things we ultimately don't want.

We have the power to keep our environment the same or change it. We have personally created it. Like chefs in the kitchen, we create the pot of stew that's in our lives: The Drama Stew.

It starts with a recipe – one that we've identified and followed, one that we've totally created ourselves, or one that's been handed down to us. Sometimes it's a blend of a couple of recipes that we make our own.

Then we exist in the safety of what we have created because we have taken great time and effort to simmer to its fullest flavor. When drama arrives in our lives, it is hard to see that it's our doing and part of our drama recipe. No outside influences are to blame. We choose to incorporate all the specific ingredients into the recipe. We put the people, circumstances and things we want in our lives into our stews. They are our ingredients.

So when the recipe we've chosen isn't giving us our desired result, we stir it, and stir it, and stir it some more to see if we can get it to taste better to us, more to our liking. Even after stirring, we realize it's still not tasting so good.

There are some recipes, ones handed down to us, that aren't delightful to make (and we certainly don't prefer). Yet, we were told along the way from someone – usually an adult when we were young – that "this is the way it's done and this is the way you will do it too."

Oh, now this is where it starts to get good. We then take this recipe – the one that doesn't meet our personal needs at all – and we recreate it without putting in our own special touches. We make it over and over and over again, hoping each time that it will be better than the last mix, but it never gets better. Instead, it becomes a pot of confusion that has no flavor and doesn't fuel passion in our lives. Still, we get used to it, and so we stir, hoping that it will become better. Then we stir again! One more time, we time stir the pot! We get the same result – the one that doesn't make us feel any better.

Here's an example: I was listening to a story from a client that sounded just like a story she had told me before – more than once. Drama in her life. Over and over again, it was the same story but in different sequence. What she was really telling me was "I'm in the same pot of stew, I just stirred the pot and this is what it looked like today." Hmmm... very interesting.

I asked her, "What about that flavor of stew is so attractive to you, if you don't really like to eat it?"

Her answer would always be the same. "I don't know. I don't like the ingredients (people) at all. "

"Really? Well, you made it," I would say.

Do you know what would always come out? (Get Ready): "I didn't make it. Everyone else in the pot keeps messing up my life. It's not what I want. I try to change but it never works. "

Remember, hard as it is to hear, you own the recipe for your Drama Stew. Did you make it? Yes! Did you decide to keep it? Yes! Did you decide to freeze the leftovers in containers for a meal at a later date? Yes! But do you have to? No!

Here's the kicker: You can change the recipe to make it right for you. The challenge you have in front of you is to detox from the drama and stop making bad stew.

idi Tip: Start detoxing your life (stew) today. The most important step in getting rid of drama is personal awareness. The fastest way to clean our own house is becoming aware that it needs to be cleaned. Often we are just used to situations, so we miss the need to clean. What areas of your life could use a cleanse? Think about it. What areas would you be able to label it as having drama in them? Start to evaluate them.

2

CHALLENGES

Do not ask for an easier life; ask to be a stronger person.
— Unknown

Let's talk for a minute about challenges. Look at this guy in the picture, hitting his head against the wall. Now that's a challenge. If you were to consider the list of all the challenging experiences in your life, what would you remember most about them? That they were fun, helpful, empowering, exciting? Probably not, but isn't that what they really were? Do you notice that when you look back on the list of great things that happened in your life, they inevitably were the result of overcoming a challenge?

As I take a walk back down Memory Lane, I can recall my greatest challenges in vivid detail, as if they are videos with color, sound, taste and smell. For example, if I had to tell you what happened during each of my mountain climbing expeditions, I could. I could give you a list of all the things packed in my backpack, as well as what I used to take the first step on the ascent to the last step at the end of the climb.

Why do I remember those details so clearly? Because those experiences are the ones that built me and shaped me. I now see that no matter how many mountains I climb (literally and figuratively), each journey gives me wisdom for the next challenge waiting. I can integrate the wisdom from that experience into my life and use it as a tool for the future.

In my real-life mountain-climbing experiences, I always had a choice: to stay safe at the bottom and avoid the experience or to go for it, to trust the experience to be just that: an experience.

Each mountain, each challenge, has its own flavor and specific lesson waiting to be learned. We can keep walking around the base aimlessly wandering to find the answer or we can climb to the top and enjoy each step.

Sometimes we're tempted to avoid experiences because all mountains look alike: "I've tried it before, and it didn't work." Instead of checking each one out and seeing its special gifts, we avoid it because of the fear that it just possibly could be the same as the last challenging climb.

When that happens, are we that afraid of the experience or ourselves? It is not the mountain that scares us: it is questioning our ability to climb the mountain. I believe we are so attached to the possible outcome of what we think the experience will bring that we avoid the new experience to stay safe.

However, at the end of the journey we will see that the answer – and the experience – is always less painful than we anticipated. Our brains (or our egos, shall I say) are wired to save us from a state of fear. There is that little voice that tells us, "This could potentially hurt, so *don't do it.*"

Then we avoid the experience, which if we had gone on would have worked out and in ways we never imagined. Don't we always arrive at a final destination over time, whether we planned it or not? We just have to decide if we will do it with lots of drama or minimal drama or no drama. Simply put, start walking and know you will get to the peak, don't question HOW. Things will work themselves out. Sometimes you just have to have courage.

In my years of coaching, I have become astonished by the simple act of encouragement. Telling people they can do it can change their lives! When clients are confronted with a challenge and they hear from me that I believe they will overcome the challenge, their inability to start climbing ceases and they begin to march ahead.

Was it my encouragement? Or, was it simply that I revealed what they already had inside: the ability to do it with or without my encouragement? We all have the ability to persevere. We all have the ability to change and grow. We all have the ability to remove our fears that block our forward progress. You can detox from the drama. You can change the recipe. You can stop making bad stew and start making good stew.

So, let me ask you a few questions: When life hands you circumstances, people or things (a recipe) that you aren't so fond of, do you have to use the recipe you have been given? No! If you choose to use it, do you have to make it exactly as it has been given to you? No! Aren't all recipes adaptable? Yes! I have learned from my kids there are lots of ingredients you can leave out of recipes and still produce an end result that is actually quite delicious.

When you choose *not* to continue to use the old recipe that doesn't work for you, it will be – you guessed it – time to get a new recipe. There's nothing wrong with the other one, it's just the wrong one for you. I know what you're thinking, "Start over? Are you kidding? This is a perfectly good pot of stew. I can't just throw it out. I have so much time invested in it. And oh, how much work it will be to find new ingredients and slice and dice and flavor it to the way I want it to be."

If you don't get a new recipe or adapt the old one, the story continues just as it is. Your life will not change. This is your drama with all the ingredients representing all the people and situations in your life. Remember what we learned from the last chapter: When the ingredients don't serve the right purpose to enhance our world, things start to taste funny. We go ahead and give them a big stir to make things interesting, or better. We move a person or situation to a different place. It's not gone. It's just moved around for a bit till it comes around again.

This works, for a short time, until the drama begins to get out of hand and comes to a boil. Things have been stirred up so many times that it seems like every ingredient – every aspect of your life – begins to boil.

Still, nothing has changed but your energy level. You are beginning to get run down from repositioning the same ingredients that never worked for you in the first place. Then, your exhaustion starts to affect your happiness. This is a pure drama recipe, no matter which way you stir it.

So, what's the problem? Well, are you ready to hear this? The main ingredient in the drama is *You*! If you weren't in it, you wouldn't have to stir the pot – or be involved in it in any way – because it wouldn't have any effect on you. You would be removed from all the drama. You would have a chance to try a new recipe.

Can you see how starting a new recipe and way of life with fewer ingredients from others' recipes and more from your own taste buds would be much more enjoyable? When you like all the ingredients, you won't have to stir them up. You could really enjoy your recipe and enjoy the ingredients that improve over time. It's certainly possible. Because we are humans, it is tough to be patient and allow life to show us the right recipes, but it's worth it.

Start understanding the drama in your life by stopping the stirring and getting out of the pot. Develop an outside perspective. This gives you greater understanding of what flavors in your life are truly sweet and which are bitter. Once you can distance yourself from the situation, you can then start straining the bitter flavors from the pot and enjoying the sweetness in your life.

Seeing it from an observing point of view – instead of being a participant – does two good things: it gives you a greater perspective on what to do with the stew (your life) and makes digesting the meal much easier, as you take one bite at a time. When you start small, you can understand what you enjoy and don't enjoy.

You have a challenge in front of you: Do you want to change an ingredient or start fresh? Look at each ingredient. Some you automatically *know* you should remove from the pot. You can begin to replace them with healthier, wiser, more enjoyable ingredients.

With your outside perspective, you can see what you have created. You can see where you've chosen to put your attention. Don't feel guilty about the things you're giving less attention to. This isn't avoidance; it is self-love. By putting the ingredients in your stew that you want and spending time with those ingredients, you create a loving, sweeter environment for yourself.

After replacing those you don't want or need, you won't have to stir the pot anymore. You just have to give your new ingredients time to meld together.

So I guess what I'm trying to say is this:

- Life is less complicated than you make it.
- Stepping out of your stew helps you stop stirring and allows everything to simmer down.
- You can live your life without getting melted into someone else's Drama Stew by focusing on your own life and cooking up your own sweet personal recipe.
- Trust in the process. It will always turn out just as it was meant to. The hardest part of a meal is smelling the aroma of the pot and having to wait until it's done. You know that you want to eat now, but it isn't ready till it cooks for a while. Practicing patience allows each ingredient in your life to show you its purpose in your life and will give you all you need to cook up the perfect meal.

idi Tip: When the drama in your life is boiling, get a piece of paper out and draw a circle on it. Then write all the ingredients currently in your life, good and bad. Put a big X on the outside of the circle (representing you and your outside perspective). Choose to see all these ingredients as individuals, things, and experiences. As the X on the outside, you can begin to address each ingredient inside the circle, one at a time. Then you can take out the bitter, unhealthy ingredients until you have a simpler stew, one that you could enjoy.

When you put it on paper, you take it out of your head, which relieves you of that mental drama.

3

THE STUFF INSIDE OF US

Self-knowledge gives a deeper understanding of others. The deeper you go in self-understanding, the more completely you will understand everyone. —Swami Kriyanand

Now, let's talk about the stuff inside us that helps us make the decisions about what is meant to be and who will share our wonderful lives with us.

Inside? That's where you are supposed to look? Why didn't anyone tell me? So many questions, I know. This is where it all gets so complicated; yet, it's simple. So many of us are searching, searching, searching for more, looking outside of ourselves for the answers to who we are, who we should love, where we fit, and what we should do. We really should be looking inside, but sometimes we are our worst critics. Then we just start self-defeating behavior, and that is no fun when you are truly trying to become a better person.

So what does it take to see ourselves clearly? What is the simplest way to walk through this life without judging ourselves for our mistakes and what we've done wrong? Is that what they are, mistakes?

Here I go again, more questions. Let me tell you how I discovered the answer: One day, it came to me that I had been asking myself the wrong questions! In the past, each time a hardship was in front of me, I would turn on "victim mode," like I was the victim of this terrible event outside of myself. I kept asking, "Why did this happen to me?" when the real questions I should have been asking were: "What can I learn from this and how is this making me better?" What a difference! You might think, "Is it that easy?" Yep!

So if just asking better questions is how we can begin to make grand changes in our lives, we all can do it. When asking empowering questions, we most often get empowering answers.

Yes, the drama that unfolds in everyone's *external* world is going on whether we all choose to engage or not. But the drama taking place inside you doesn't need to be there. We are all the creators of our lives. Ask yourself, what would you want to do to be happier right now if you could? What would you want to get rid of or release?

Following my divorce, I finally asked myself "What do I want?" I was not blaming my ex-husband for why my life wasn't sweet. He had his own pot of stew to deal with and I had to stop expecting him make my stew taste better. It wasn't his responsibility. It was mine. Yes, that was a hard lesson to learn: it is not others' responsibility to make me happy. It's my responsibility to go inside and ask what I want.

It was up to me to make some tough and possibly intimidating changes that would, at the end of the experience, bring me happiness. I chose that path, and it did bring me happiness. Now it's your turn.

idi Tip: Can you think of one thing you would like to turn from frustration and bitterness into contentment? One thing, one person, one situation, or just one plaguing thought that if you changed your ways, the situation would change too. Be honest with yourself. You don't have to explain it to others; you just have to explain it to yourself to make your insides happy. Acknowledging it is all it takes to start making it reality. It may take some time, though, so remember patience.

4

THE STUFF OUTSIDE OF US

What other people think of me is none of my business. One of the highest places you can get to is being independent of the good opinions of other people. - Dr. Wayne Dyer

We can almost title this chapter "Rules and Relationships," because that's what we'll be talking about. Both of these are in fact, outside of us – they are delicious outside influences that we regularly incorporate into our Drama Stew.

We can create the base for our healthy stew with happy insides. The place where *our answers* are found is inside. The place where we find *the lessons that reveal the answers* are outside. Rules and relationships are the misunderstood influences; we mistake them for ways to bring us internal happiness. They are really interruptions we need to make us question what we want. Let's take a minute to talk about the first part.

RULES

"Rules, rules, rules. All we have are Rules!" This is what came out of my daughter's mouth at the dinner table following a discussion on how important it was to eat a balanced diet. That night, I opened my mind to see the world through her eyes. Were my rules the right ones for her? Were the rules positive, but the approach wrong for her? Would certain tasks easier for her to accomplish with her own format and timeline? Who decided three meals per day are the perfect solution for her body?

I neglected to see the perfection in her current eating habits: small amounts of grains, fruits, and vegetables throughout the day. She is so amazing, so perfect in her own way. I was too busy just spouting out the rules of society at dinner: she should clean her plate, even though the portions I served her were too large in the first place.

Rules are part of our every moment – they guide our behavior. The unfortunate result of rules is that you run the risk of getting programmed with another person's rules. There are rules that are right for you and others that are not. Be on the lookout: you'll find yourself in different situations with different rules, and you'll have to make decisions about what to do. If rules you encounter don't embrace the form of love, kindness and compassion you're comfortable with, then they may not be the best for you to follow. Just ask yourself, "Who made these rules I am following, and are they right for me?" Go inside and evaluate them against your personal moral code.

Why is it so easy for us to follow others' rules at times? Why are there other moments when we throw caution to the wind? Sometimes we just want to embrace the moment because the joy and freedom that comes from no rules or expectations is exhilarating. When we do that, there are no judgments, expectations or results necessary to appreciate the joy flowing through us.

So we need to take time for that occasionally. Think about the last time you chose to not follow the rules. For some of us, it may have been never, but for others of us it may have been an hour ago.

Can you see how the concept of rules affects us all? Rules can both help us and hinder us. There is a distinct difference between living with passion and living a life drained by walking on a societal path that we think we are expected to follow when it's not right for us.

The things we have passion for are easy to identify because they unleash emotions of joy, gratitude, desire, fulfillment and fun. This passion can be for any part of life: a job, a hobby, a person or a place. We could spend 20 out of 24 hours per day doing it and have no need for rest because the passionate experience fills up our energy faster than we can expend it. It's a place where we are OK in solitude because we can get preoccupied and nothing else matters. Other rules may have little effect on us during these moments because we are living within the rules of the passionate experience.

Don't misunderstand the other rules I am addressing. Yes, you still need to stop at a red light, follow the speed limit, and pay your bill after your meal. Those are laws that keep us all moral. I am focusing on the rules we are taught or that we make up to feel connected and in control.

These are the rules in your head that guide your thinking that things MUST be a certain way to be safe, like:

- "Everyone in my family is a general contractor. Therefore, I will be one when I grow up too. This is the way it has always been, so it must be true for me, when actually I would love to be an accountant. "

- "I was abused as a child so I will accept an abusive relationship. It is what I know and feels right for me.
- I have never received unconditional love, and therefore I refuse to give it. "

- "I am a single, 36 year-old so it is time to marry. I must choose a partner before I get too old. "

Do any of these sound familiar? We incorporate these rules and add them to our Drama Stew. Here's another example: by society's rules, I thought a business degree was a good solid foundation to prepare me for my career. I began my college experience as a business major. I could barely function. I almost dropped out two years into the process because I was so unhappy. The classes were draining, boring, and no fun. I wasn't in tune with my intuition at that point, but my mother saw that I needed to make a change or I was done.

I realized that I needed healing as my focus. After I changed my degree from business to science (which added time and more classes to getting my degree), I noticed that all the extra effort and time to catch up were more energizing than 10 minutes in my prior business classes. This intrigued me and made me smile.

We all listen to society's rules, so if you're on a high horse, get off it and be straight with yourself for a second. We look at others and think like this: "If I can buy a fancy car, then I am a successful lawyer." Or, "If I can save enough lives, then I am worthy of being called a doctor." Or, "If I can feed enough underprivileged people, then I am a compassionate person."

If, Then. These scenarios are part of the lines everyone tries to tell themselves so they can feel better on the inside. That's not really the case, though. In truth, if you are a lawyer who clears one wrongly-accused victim, you are successful. If you are a doctor who saves one life, you are a great doctor. If you feed one person with loving encouragement and supportive words, you are compassionate. But somewhere along the road we picked up societal rules telling us at what point we are considered successful or acceptable.

Wait a second. Who gave society the title of Your Rule Maker, anyway? Success isn't a destination; it's something you are – today and every day!

So when school, jobs, people, hobbies or anything exhausts you, evaluate the relationships and the rules. Maybe it is time to allow your compass needle to turn in a new direction. You'll be attracted to the true purpose of your life through the things that bring you that joy and passion. Just acknowledge that you desire passion in your life – that's all it takes to draw it to you.

However, if the external rules you work within are draining you, you are experiencing a wrong choice. Most likely, it is someone else's choice. When you realize this, it could be hugely impactful in your life. For instance, what if you have been a seamstress your whole life and realize you didn't have to be? What if you saw that it was just a family rule, when you would rather be a nurse and still could be? Even the knowledge of this is freeing – you don't have to be a seamstress anymore! When you have that kind of realization, know it's not too late to make a change. You can go out and study to be a nurse. Yes, it will take commitment and time, but don't allow the sacrifice it would take for you to become a nurse to override the passion you have for doing it.

Ask yourself what brings you passion? The answer will emerge. It may not be in that immediate moment, but it will reveal itself, likely in a form you wouldn't expect. The perfection in acknowledging that you want more passion in your life is what may lead you in a new direction, down a new path.

Remember, every new path traveled has a few weeds and rocks on it. But pay attention to them, because they are there to help you stay on path. These hold lessons: some may cause you to pause and raise a brow, and others may just be to validate your passion. Small weeds and rocks are minor details in comparison to a dead end where you could have been walking in circles or a base camp where you don't start the climb. As we said earlier, you can stay the base of the mountain or you can break your rules and begin your ascent with one step up.

RELATIONSHIPS

This brings us to the second part of the chapter, the relationship part, where rules and relationships meet. Oh no – can you feel it? More questions are coming.

Think about these:

- What is your relationship like with your kids? Is it loving and encouraging? How do you communicate? Is yelling at your kids OK as a form of communication with them? Is that a rule that you were taught by someone? Is it the right way to communicate with *your* own children, in *your* house? Maybe, maybe not. The key is to not do it just because that's what you were taught and that's how you think it should be, without considering how each child learns and what will help him/her grow. Oftentimes, some yell when they are experiencing stress from another direction, not from the children, and they don't deserve us taking it out on them.

- What is your relationship with your finances? A major stressor in many people's lives is money. When you are spinning your wheels financially, ask yourself, "What rules I have made for myself that are stopping me from asking for the necessary help to be free of these worries?" For example, do you have the rule that says owning a home makes you successful," even though financially it is drowning you? The learning lesson in that moment may be that it's just not the right home for you. Always look at your other options – in this case you could rent, get a hotel room, or stay with friends or family. There are always other ways; you may just have to look a little harder for them.

- When you are interacting with your spouse or partner, what rules do you have that determine what a good spouse should be? Who taught you *Good Spouse Rules*...Are they his/her rules as well? If you are having a conflict with each other, maybe it's time to ask if your rules are interfering. Does the spouse know what rules you have attached to the standard in your head of a good spouse?

Before we talk about spousal rules, let's take a step back and think about why our partners and spouses are there in the first place. Partners enter our lives at various stages. They are the markers of what we are at that moment, and our relationships are the makers of what type of lives we will live. When most of us are searching for love, the last thing we consider is learning how this new man or woman is a true symbol of our current place in lIfe. We don't realize we are attracting a mirror image of ourselves. It scares us all to think this, but it's so true.

Many women have fairytale images of what relationships will be: You know – the strong, independent, supportive and protective knight in shining armor sitting on top a white horse who rides by and sweeps them off their feet.

Well, looking back over 20 years of relationships, instead I see donkeys carrying what could be characterized as men, but in no way did these men have knight-like qualities. The one thing I did not experience was being swept off my feet by those guys. Instead, I've been taught by them. That's right, *taught*. The greatest lessons I would learn in life would come from *men*. Who would have guessed it? Well, guys, I am now giving you credit for the gifts you have given me. I'll bet you need some more explanation about this.

Men, you see that women are character builders for you as well, right? What teaches us the biggest lessons in our lives? I looked inside and realized it was the relationships that I have had the pleasure of experiencing. That's exactly what their purpose was: to teach me and give me a direct experience that was necessary for my growth. It wasn't that they were in my life to hurt or help me; they were there to build me as a person. They were present until I learned the lesson they were there to teach. When the lesson was learned, they either disappeared or stayed to keep pushing me to become even wiser in the lesson.

The part I kept missing was accepting them as an experience and not as an interruption. Accepting the gifts being brought to me by experience was their reason for being in my life. Allowing myself to receive these gifts without attachment to how they would teach it taught me to learn the lesson.

Each time a new person came into my life (especially the ones I thought were there to hurt me – you know, the ones who bring you tears, the ones who touch your soul), I began to see they were there to strengthen me. I had to choose to see their presence for its perfection of making me better, not making me less, which is what many of us do.

So what are the lessons being given to you by the current relationships in your life? That is up to you to decide. Will you receive the experience and the learning or not? This is part of the Drama Detox. Realize that all your relationships (the business partners, lovers, friends, kids and acquaintances) come into your life for their purpose of teaching you a new piece of wisdom. You may not have gained this wisdom without them being present.

Allow the current relationships in your life to teach you acceptance, knowledge, intimacy, love, empowerment, trust, fun, connection, or just joy. Allow them to give you the lesson so they can receive the same in return from you. Allow them to push you past your internal fears. You'll be surprised about the lessons you learn and the gifts you receive.

Relationships themselves are truly gifts, but we have to get back to the earlier "spousal rules discussion. Imagine this scenario: The door to the kitchen flies open. She comes in: her arms are full from picking up dinner, the dry cleaning, the kids' art from the day and all her business paperwork to be finished that evening (following dinner, bath time, homework, bed time stories, back rubs and lullabies). She sees him on the computer playing a video game, not having completed any of the items she asked of him in their prior telephone conversation.

Can you see it steaming inside of her? She is now running down a list of all the rules she has in her head of a good spouse and which ones he has currently broken, which she adds to the list of previously broken rules that sits in the archived files of her brain.

Here we go – the White Picket Fence Rules to follow that make your marriage/relationship successful.

We can go back in time to the 60s TV show *Leave It to Beaver*, about the All-American Family. Beaver's mom always had dinner waiting for the family and kept a perfectly clean home. To top it off, she dressed impeccably with not one hair out of place. Do you remember Beaver's mom ever greeting her husband as the woman in the earlier scenario just did? No! Nor did you ever see her taking on tasks outside of tending to her home or children (no other employment, friendships, or hobbies). No wonder she had time to put on pearls to vacuum. But is this behavior, these rules for governing a house, realistic?

Now fast forward to today... two working parents with full time positions, balancing household responsibilities. Many parents have children in daycare, adding to the expenses which are pulling on them financially. Yet, during this whole experience, half a century later, we all keep trying to follow rules of the past. We chose to do all these things in a day to fit the 1960s world into today's world. No wonder it doesn't always work.

Our rules cage us from experiencing life in peace. To add to matters, we have now decided on rules for others to be in our lives. The funny thing is we don't tell them about these rules. We just expect them to know. This is particularly true with spouses. We expect them to behave according to our rules, from whatever time period or whatever point of view we're coming from.

You have to remember you are living in your world and not your spouse's world. Spouses aren't thinking about all the things you did today. They are evaluating their own situation according to their own personal set of rules. Being upset with a spouse is your choice because you feel all these things in your head are important. You made these priorities so you have no right to be upset when your spouse doesn't fulfill your needs your way – that they didn't follow *your* rules. I know that's hard to hear. Step outside of yourself and determine what would allow you to both see the same picture. Think about how you can best communicate with each other.

Here's an idea: just for fun, start a conversation by saying: "Are you Psychic or a Master of Communication?" Of course, the answer will most likely be no to both, but it will give you an opening to talk about your spousal rules.

Ask yourself if your rules are logical and filled with love, kindness and compassion? Sometimes just recognizing that it is time to let go of a situation – no matter how significant it may seem at the moment – is what allows us to let go of the rules we have. We can evaluate why they were so important in the first place. The rules are usually set of from a disillusioned fairytale image in our head. Be honest with yourself on why they are in your life. You will get the answer. If people, places or situations are meant to be in your life they will return ten times over without effort.

Ask yourself what rules you have created in your life as forms of protection. Do these rules keep you safe and in control? Or are they stopping you from expressing your true soul and encouraging more suffering than necessary? The reality is that we have no control: "Everything and everyone happens for a reason."

When we accept each moment in time as a lesson and gift, we are no longer tied down and controlled by the rules. So never question where you are at any given moment in time, only question if it is not bringing you joy, peace and love. You can stand in your power of just being present and 100 percent with your authentic self. Your authentic self might mean doing things your way. Let's talk about "your way" for a minute.

Remember the permission we discussed earlier, when I believed in others for what they want to do and gave them permission to do, say and be what they want and they did? Well, ask what you want your authentic self to express without concern if others like it.

This leads us to another question... Who's way is it? This way, that way, my way, your way or the highway? It's time to see that all ways lead to the final destination. Just because you see it one way, doesn't mean that the rule you have for doing it is right. If you want it done that way, do it yourself or let it go. You will still get to the end of the road, no matter whose set of rules you use. Ultimately it is up to you to tame your internal suffering if others aren't following your personal rules. There is no need to suffer, simply remember their rules don't come close to yours, so stop expecting them to follow yours and your suffering will decrease.

Getting there with fewer rules just helps get you there with less drama. I am asking you to break your own rules on what is OK for you to live the life you want. Even better, don't break anything, just say out loud every day, "There are no rules." These outside influences can help you accomplish what you want to accomplish. They can help you to be who you want to be for the life you want to live.

idi Tip: This was a long chapter, given that relationships are a potent part of our lives and help build our character. When evaluating relationships, use this simple scale: if it makes you cry, it might be time to say goodbye. If it makes you smile, do what it takes to keep it.

PART II:
MAKING CHANGES

5

STORIES AND SWEAR WORDS

We don't see things as they are, we see things as we are.
—Anais Nin

Don't you just love a juicy story – one all filled with drama, adventure, anticipation and surprise! This little chapter about stories and swear words could be the most important part of this book. So, I really just have to give it to you straight: Every challenge you are experiencing, in any part of your life, is a story. What you say about it is a story which you can change. OK, that's it! Next!

Is it that easy to make self-transformation possible in your life? Yes, you can do it yourself. However, I am a strong advocate for asking a non-judgmental person (counselor, coach or anyone who doesn't have emotional connection to you) for support. They are the ones who can get past your story and reveal the real source of your struggle.

So you want to hear a little more? OK. It's your story why you can't do something. I must throw this in: *Can't* is the other swear word in my home. Funny, right? My girls will sometimes say, "Mommy, Sissy said a swear word." "Really, what did she say?" I'll ask. "She said the C-word," she'll reply.

I know what you are thinking — that there are other swear words could start with a c. Yes, but get your head straight. This one, *can't*, should be considered a swear word. Simply don't say it, ever! If it is not part of your vocabulary, you won't give yourself the option.

OK, so back to stories. You know them well:

- "I can't lose weight "
- "I can't find a job."
- "I can't go to school."
- "I can't fix my marriage."
- "I can't stop smoking, drinking, drugs, sex, spending, shopping, etc. "

The list is limitless. Whichever poison you pick, it can easily be preceded with "I can't" and followed by "I have tried everything and nothing works. I seem to go backwards not forward."

I can't, I can't. Have you heard this famous quote by Henry Ford: "Whether you think you can, or think you can't, you're right"? That's right! You will come up with every excuse in the book as to why you can't, which is just avoiding responsibility. Yes, you heard me right, avoidance of responsibility. That's what can't really means. There's not just one but a whole list of stories why we are not able to accomplish the things we want in our lives.

We usually pick them up somewhere while growing up, and then decide that whomever we learned them from knew what they were talking about. Therefore, they must be true.

Why didn't we question them? Because we were young, with immature brains. We were unable to decipher which of the stories told to us by adults were true/not true. We thought that since they were the boss, surely they must be right, *right*? No. That's *not* right! But now you've grown up, and some of those true/not true stories are still with you as if they are true for you today.

As an adult, they can be a tremendous source of frustration. You can keep running into situations you can't explain until you look closely at their origins.

Look at this list:

What you question:	What's really going on:
Why doesn't anyone seem to get me?	I didn't/don't get me.
Why doesn't anyone love me for me?	I didn't/don't love me for me.
Why don't any of the weight loss options work for me?	I wasn't willing to gain the belief that I deserved a beautiful, fit, lean body.
Why doesn't anyone want to help me?	I wasn't willing to help myself.

Do any of these sound familiar? So when you are frustrated with a situation, simply ask yourself a couple of questions: "What is the story you have associated with it?" "Is the story one you have heard from an adult when you were young?" "Do you have absolute proof that it's the truth?"

Here's a common example: When I was little, I had an uncle tell me (as I was entering the ripe stage of puberty) that I would be *fat* when I grew up.

You see where this is going, right? Clearly, this is a setup for later. You can guess what would become the biggest fear I had going through the growing pains of becoming a woman. I began to believe the story "I'm fat." Was it true? No! Did I have proof that I would become fat? No! Did he even have proof that I would become fat? No! Was his story true? Not At All!

Yet I struggled with my weight for almost 30 years.

Then I asked myself the question, "Where did this fear of fat come from?" It came from someone who had no knowledge of this truth. Nor was he trying to intentionally hurt me in any way. I finally saw the real situation. There it was, like a red flashing light saying, "Hello, Gorgeous!" It simply was not true.

The truth is I am a small, fit, healthy, beautiful woman. Was I finally willing to let it go and now settle in with the truth? Absolutely. The day I decided to become who I wanted to be and not what I feared becoming, I did! If deciding to want to be fit and lean is possible just by deciding, what else do I want? It's that easy – you can do it just by saying, "I can!"

I have yet to hear someone come to me and say "I can" and not do it. Talking about can should be fun since it's a bit more scary than the swear word. Can means – you guessed it – the opposite of can't: *responsibility*. When you say it in conjunction with any topic, you give yourself the understanding that failure is not an option, and:

- That you will give yourself the gift of receiving,
- That all resources are available, and
- That you have the answer *within* you to get it.

There it is again – Within. Hmmm, didn't anyone tell you how amazing and brilliant you are? You do have all the answers, even to the challenging situations in your life.

Often, when we find ourselves in a sticky situation we start to analyze outside influences as possible culprits. Well, now, that's definitely *not* a sign of taking responsibility. We can find the true culprits inside, as well as the solutions.

64

Why are we so afraid of looking inside? Because if we see it, oh no...others might too and that would ruin everything, *right*? So, let's just consider (for the moment) we keep all the scary stuff under wraps and keep a lid on what we are struggling with internally. This is such a typical human response, to protect our soft little insides. In truth, we have the power to create our environments and accomplish the things we believe we can.

idi Tip: What story do you tell yourself that has *can't* in it? Give yourself permission to live in the truth of now and create a new story with "I can" today.

6

DREAMS

Live out of your imagination, not your history. -
Stephen Covey

The next time someone tells you, "You're dreaming," respond back with "*Yes, I am* and I intend to fulfill each and every one of my dreams!" As we grow older, our dreams get very, very, very small. Then, for some of us, they disappear altogether. Isn't that sad? What do we have to look forward to after we have no more dreams?

Think about dreams for a minute. So what are dreams? Do they just happen when you go to sleep or do they happen while you're awake too? The answer is both. It depends on how you look at them.

I would like to consider dreams to be wishes, because our society has somehow become dream squashers, where wishes are more accepted than dreams. People are often questioned for chasing their dreams. Having a dream can seem to have a stigma attached to it, like it isn't realistic or it isn't possible.

Instead of talking about what your dreams are, we can talk about what your wishes are. "What do you wish for in your life?" is a better question to ask than "What do you dream about?" Can you imagine this scene: A genie shows up out of the blue, offering you a wish. What would you wish for? In our little scene, consider this a very important genie. She's not like others, where you only get three wishes and that's it. This genie will keep granting wishes on one condition: you keep constant vigil on your wishes. You work to make them happen. This genie is like a best friend who encourages, promotes, and pushes you to live the wishes you asked for without allowing you to listen to outside dream squashers because honestly, aren't they everywhere?

Family, friends, co-workers, and strangers want their wishes to be granted too, which could interfere with your wishes. Or, you may see those others settling for a wish-less life. Does that mean that you should too? No! Your ability to wish is not connected to anyone else's ability or desire to dream. You can do it all on your own. And you should.

Let's go back to your genie. We'll call her the "Universal Genie." Now imagine this Universal Genie appears and says, "As long as you keep wishing beyond your limiting beliefs, I will encourage you to make it happen." Suddenly, you realize that each and every wish is attainable. If this happened, would you start wishing? If you knew without a doubt that the wish was possible, would you do it? Nothing is beyond your grasp in this world if your mind can hold onto the vision of it – whether it is a thing, concept, idea, or experience.

Over the years, I have asked many people to share their wishes and dreams with me. Every one of us has desires, and they are different than those of the next person.

When I ask for a description of wishes with pictures, words, or concepts the picture is completely different person to person. You would think everyone would want to have the common dreams appearing in media: to travel the world, to have better health, to be in loving relationships, to own fast cars, to have supportive friends, or to take a vacation on the beach. We all wish for some version of these, but not in the same form as the next person. The car, home, relationship, career, etc. that you dream of, and wish for, is entirely different from the dream of your neighbor, sibling, friend or parent. It is unique to you.

Somewhere during our growing up years, family members handed down their hopes, wishes and dreams. These were theirs, unique to them, and sadly, not all of those are in line with ours as adults. As children, we think adults know best. We take these hopes, wishes and dreams and then accept them as our own. But as we get older, we can question them. If you ask yourself, "Are these hopes, wishes and dreams mine?" You might surprise yourself by the answer you have *within.*

This is the interesting part. Many of my clients have just needed someone to give them permission to start dreaming their own dreams again – to release the other people's dreams and concentrate on what they desire. So today, I give you permission to begin wishing again. It starts simply by getting back to the idea that it's possible to have what you want.

Uh oh, that's a scary place, isn't it? What do you want? If you actually said it, you might have to start living it. What might others think? Yes, you can hear the words from the naysayers right now: "You're dreaming! Stop!"

Don't you dare!

I am here to say I have had some wild wishes, and I will admit at some point in my life that I said "I could never do that!" Then I ended up in situations where I didn't have a choice except to do it.

There was a point when I said I will *never* get divorced. Yep! Did it! I said I will *never* have my own hair salon. Yep! Did it! I said I will *never* write a book. Yep! Did it! These are just a few examples. Later, I came to realize that *never* was in my head because society said those things were for others, not me.

I had no business doing those things because I didn't have the education or experience to do so. Then I came to realize that if I can dream it, I can do it. Accomplishing those goals, however big or small, stomped out the idea of *never* in me.

So what's stopping us? Time was the factor that I realized was the big wish squasher. For most people, it's easy to say, "I don't have time." If we see a thing as too time-consuming, it must be outside of our capacity. We think we can never do it because we don't have time to do so. The reality is that time is the least important factor in the equation. *Wishing for something* starts the clock of when you will finish it. Seeing the clock is a reminder every day of where we want to go and not where we have come from.

I have dream boards, books, papers and sticky notes everywhere in my world reminding me of what I wish for. For instance, writing this book is a creation of my daughter's G-shaped sticky notes. They're everywhere in our home – on the bathroom mirror, shower door, this computer I'm typing on, the car steering wheel, the light switches, door handles – yes everywhere. They say, "Finish publishing next book."

Here's the background of that. For a few years, I have been asked to write the work I do with clients into a book. The task seemed daunting, given all that I have on my plate. Still, every time I would sit down or walk anywhere in my home, there was the reminder of what was possible in small chunks of time (There's that time thing again). I thought, "OK, if my wish is meant to be, it can happen over time, just not immediately. It will come out in my own words with a chapter every now and then."

Am I a writing expert? Not even close. Do I have an editor as I write this? No. Will others want to read it? No clue! Do I care about becoming a best-selling author? Not sure. But, do I have a wish to get it out and put it on paper? Absolutely. How I do it is not as important as what I do. Maybe that means I will self-publish, ask my mom to edit, and count on my clients as the only readers. It's just my wish to create a book, and I want all the G-shaped sticky notes to come down...Ha ha.

Maybe a little part of me wants to show myself that I can do it. That it's easier than it seemed. Then I can tell myself, "Well, there is another wish down. OK, Universal Genie, what's next?"(Remember, this genie keeps granting wishes as long as you keep making them. When one comes true, no need to stop there! Hmmm, now this can be fun, exciting, and inspiring. All I have to do is go inside and ask a simple question, "What do I want?"

Our dreams, wishes, capabilities and joys are always inside us. If we take a moment to start dreaming and wishing for a life that seems to excite a passion inside, the rest starts to unfold all by itself.

As I said before, the *how* part is not important... It's the *what* that is most important. You see, most people stop the wishing process because the *how* gets in the way. It's like a giant taking his big boot and giving it a smash. I am tempted to consider *how* as a swear word, but it does serve its purpose when we ask other types of questions to educate us such as: "How do you bake a cake?" "How can you drive a car?" "How do you spell a word?" So, I will only consider it a swear word if it comes in a sentence before any of your wishes. "How am I supposed to _____?" You fill in the blank. If you say it in that form, consider that you just swore. And yes, maybe for some swearing is OK. In this context, it's not the typical swear word but it does invite the giant to smash your dreaming process. Then it's *not* OK.

So now it's your turn to talk to the Universal Genie about your wishes. Ask yourself one question: "What do you want?" Then pick a dream. Start with one at a time, and look at them together. You will see they all begin to overlap. They become part of you, showing you what you look like inside and what you know you are capable of inside. Then all the stuff outside begins to lose its potency in your personal life. You can spend your energy focusing on your dreams, not on the stuff outside.

I am often asked what my favorite wish is. Well, this is easy to answer. I put it in my daily affirmations and prayers and I have chosen to express it as a person. I have the words unconditional love in big print on a board, sticky notes, and ingrained in my brain. This is what I wish to become and I wish for that energy to be part of me every day. I'll ask you twice about yours: First, to figure it out, and later to help you remember it. When you let go of the time constraint and the *how* constraint and focus on the outcome, things seem to work out.

By deciding what you want, it becomes easy to let go of what you don't want. So keep dreaming, keep wishing, and keep asking that Universal Genie to encourage you to make what you want happen.

idi Tip: Find a notebook, poster board, sticky notes, anything you can start documenting your grandest Dreams today. Make a list, draw pictures or cut and paste. Start now. Make big wishes and show the Universal Genie what you want!

7

FISH IN THE SEA

The sea hath fish for every man. -William Camden

After leaving our chapter on wishing for what we want, it would only seem fitting to follow with a discussion of love. We have heard the traditional basic human needs are food, water and shelter. I truly believe that love is a basic human need as well. We all search for it, cry over it, read about it, and have endless conversations about it. We are now a generation that can google it. As easy as it is to find documentation on what it is and how to find it, we all still seem to still be searching in an endless sea.

No matter what an individual's upbringing, challenges, or lifestyle is, we all want to feel loved. Right now, let's specifically focus on partners or relationships and how to find the right one for *you*.

When I ask my clients why they are not finding the right partner, it seems the answer could be a repeat recording. "I don't know. I just keep attracting the same partner. After a time, I realize that it still isn't the right one, I move on, only to encounter the same in a different person. "

Now, isn't this interesting? Then, I thought to ask them a simpler question: "What do you want in a partner? Again the common answer is, "I don't know!"

Is that true? Do we really not know what we are attracted to? Or, are we just fearful to wish for what we really want? Given that love involves emotional connection with another, we tend to settle for less so we can avoid being accountable for what we get. It's a little easier to walk away from an experience if it isn't quite right. But ultimately we do want to share our hopes, wishes, and fears with one person we truly trust.

Unfortunately, we tend to trust the wrong people out in the world – many times for the wrong reasons. Then, we end up finding out after time that it is the wrong person and we have to reset and start over. Was this person bad? Not at all, just not the right one for you. As we've said earlier, each person comes into our lives to teach us something. It's up to us to learn the lesson as we move on to the next or realize that they are there to stay.

Let's take a little journey to a tropical destination such as Hawaii. Now see the incredible blue water and imagine how many fish are in that vast ocean. You decide to take a snorkeling trip out into deeper water to see what is really out there under the surface. After the boat's crew finds a resting place for your dive, they drop anchor and encourage you to jump in and enjoy.

So, you jump in and start to view all of the incredibly beautiful fish swimming around in this clear water: Blue, red, orange, green, silver – so many colors and all equally beautiful.

Now imagine each of these fish are the available prospects of datable partners out in your current environment. As you venture out to find the perfect partner, you start to open up to see other possibilities. You can observe and compare all the amazing gifts that each person has, similar to comparing these beautiful fish you just saw in the sea. You've probably heard the expression, "There are plenty of fish in the sea."

But if you were to be more specific with your true inner wishes and dreams of your ideal partner, you might find that as lovely as the red, green and orange fish are they aren't as attractive to you as the blue ones with a little yellow and turquoise in them.

This is true in relationships. As lovely as all the individuals are out in your immediate world, it's hard to know which ones to focus on, given so much beauty at first glance. It might be less work if the field were narrowed down a bit, but we hesitate to be specific, thinking we are being too greedy or non-accepting. Doing this it allows you to want the wishes you want. It's that simple. What you wish for is never the same as what the person sitting next to you wants.

Start making your wishes more clear with your ideal mate's qualities. Decide what is most important to you. Divide the list into what is negotiable and non-negotiable. There will be 5-10 that are MUST qualities; The others are just to help you to find internal clarity on what you find attractive in another.

Instead of feeling like you are searching in an endless sea and feeling lost, you can feel less drama in the experiences. For instance, knowing you are really attracted to individuals who like to ride bicycles is big, because not everyone does. When you meet someone, you can determine quickly if they have this characteristic or not. Doing this exercise can help you to evaluate anyone who comes into your personal ocean. Be willing to see if they have the qualities you've identified. If not, going back to the bicycle example, would they be willing to learn, participate with you or make a change in their regular routine to be with you?

Go ahead wish for your ideal mate and see what starts to arrive in your space. If you are in a committed partnership, do the same exercise. Consider how many wonderful qualities are in your partner and how many are missing. We tend to focus on their challenges more than their gifts, and clearly evaluating them will help us appreciate them more or give us the courage to move on without them.

idi Tip: See if you can make a list of 100 qualities — spiritual, emotional, physical, and moral. This is a personal wish list so don't question your wants. Just know some will be adaptable when the right fish with blue, yellow and turquoise shows up.

8

ENERGY

The game of life is a game of boomerangs. Our thoughts, deeds and words return to us sooner or later with astounding accuracy.— Florence Scovel Shinn

Energy is a topic that is unseen but more real than anything. We all feel it; we just seem to give it the least focus since we cannot see it. Sometimes, it's the things we can't see that are the things we feel the most.

Quantum physics teaches that nothing is fixed, that there are no limitations, and that everything is vibrating energy. By understanding that everything is energy in a state of potential and by applying intention to bring into our lives what we focus on, it is never necessary to feel stuck with an undesirable life.

We are creators of our universe.

The physical world is a sea of energy constantly flashing into and out of existence. It is through our thoughts that we transform this ever-changing energy into an observable reality. Therefore, we can guide our reality with our thoughts. Sadly, we forget that even our poor thoughts are creating our reality. This is the drama we dislike and have to bring awareness to ongoing thoughts.

 Research shows us with quantum physics, science is embracing the notion that human beings are not powerless victims and moving toward an understanding that we are fully-empowered creators of our lives.

Einstein said, "Everything is energy and that's all there is to it... It can be no other way." This is not his philosophy, this is physics. Let's look at some science facts. Einstein's 1905 formula, $E = mc^2$ explains the relationship between energy and matter, that is, that energy and matter are interchangeable – so, in reality, everything is energy or traveling mass. Energy is simply a bunch of atoms bouncing off of each other to make something: A table, a spoon, a heart, a body – even a simple thought. So if a thought is energy, can you see it? No. Is it real? Yes.

Sometimes thoughts can be confusing or inconsistent. You might ask yourself, "Right and true are the same things aren't they?" Not really. It can be right for you, even if it is not right for another. Let's say a group of people were asked over for dinner. One said the steak dinner was delicious. This may be right on the mark for that person, but, come to find out, it was not true for another guest who does not enjoy steak. So, it was the same dinner, but different truths about the dinner.

A client recently told me, "I am not feeling right about my boyfriend, but I don't know why." Her partner was acting cold and distant. The relationship she was in was getting unstable and starting to open deep emotions within and she could feel it. That mental ping-pong we do when we allow others' drama to affect our internal world was happening to her. It was easier to question things outside of her, namely what her partner's actions meant. So I asked her to use the energy around her to give her answers so she would feel confident within. She could use some universal answers to determine if this was her pot of stew or if she was reacting to her partner's pot. Was what she was telling me about him true? She had no clue and was asking the wrong person (me) for answers. She then told me she proceeded to say a prayer, asking for her to see the real truth about the situation.

This is where we have to trust that we are all energy and that the Universe (or Higher Power, or universal energy, or God) will support you if you just ask. Say the words in your head and ask what you can do to see this situation for its truth? A solution tends to fall right into your lap if you trust it will. What she found was his actions had nothing to do with her. Her boyfriend called 30 minutes later explaining he was having health challenges that he was fearful of sharing with her. It was his pot of stew she was feeling, not her own.

Can we all do this? Absolutely! When fear starts to creep in on us, ask for assistance from the energy sources you believe in. The answers will arrive out of the blue and show up within you, so you can trust it.

We can simplify this concept with the example of a hand shake. Are there ever times when you shake someone's hand and it feels uncomfortable, and other times when it feels safe and empowering? Use that feeling to trust the energy you are picking up from another. No one is a bad person per se, they just may be carrying more than one pot of drama in their own energy field.

When you meet someone, consider this: Is this person empowering and someone you want to engage in? It is entirely up to you, but you have the power to begin to decipher what you pick up. Internally you will know what feels right for you.

When we accept others for all they are capable of and we no longer expect anything more of them, we can build a healthy relationship. If they are unable to provide what you expect from them, then that is when you know they are not capable of giving you what you deserve.

It's a little tricky. It doesn't mean they aren't capable of giving it to someone else; it's just not for you. So set them free to find that love elsewhere; then you can make an open space for a new teacher! These teachers come in so many forms (friends, lovers, employers, children, parents, strangers, animals, etc.). Be ready to acknowledge and receive them. Keep in mind, you may have another experience – just when you think your lesson is learned, a new and bigger lesson shows up from someone new.

We are on a constant path of learning. I find that I want to learn each lesson even more quickly as they arrive. I have definitely found if you don't learn it the first time, it *will* come back again and again and more challenging each time until I do learn the lesson your being taught.

Be aware of the role you play in the relationships. I find clients who like to take on the role of rescuer in relationships give until they are being pulled from their core. Then they become vulnerable to people who take advantage of their giving nature and become overly tired, sad, and lonely. They draw others who aren't giving back, just taking. They have not learned that everything that happens to us happens because we choose it and rescuing others was their choice, not the fault of those receiving the rescuing. It's the choices we make or don't make, and nothing else!

Nothing is right or wrong with any of us. I know this is hard to hear, but if you are unhappy in your relationships, it is always because something is missing in your own life. Be honest with yourself and take responsibility for what you are doing. Detox to make the world you want.

Consider a scale of feelings. When two people are in an unconditional, loving relationship, both are filled with love at 100%. Thus, when we build on that 100% and start to develop surpluses, we are still full when we give to another from our 110% because giving 5% isn't going to emotionally affect us. Thus the other person receives 5% and is now feeling their surplus as well. Now they have no concern in sending back energy to their partner who just gave to them, because they can give without being depleted below 100%.

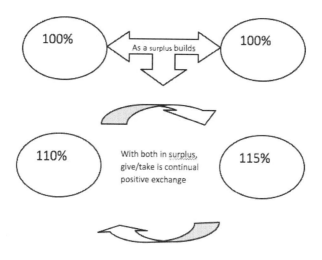

The challenge arises when a 90% person and a 50% person meet. The 50% will always be in need. The 90% will start to give because he/she feels pretty good, and then he/she will give and give, not aware of the fact that now he has become the one at 50% and the partner is now at 90%. So the push and pull begins to take place to regain the energy loss.

This transference of energy taking place is completely invisible by the way. All this is happening unconsciously, while one person in the relationship is feeling less happy and possibly resentful and they don't know why and the other is feeling more alive. Here's a pictorial view of it:

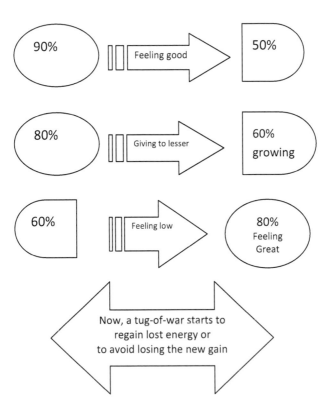

If someone is 100% and then a 60% partner shows up, he should know right away this is not good for him and find a way to disengage.

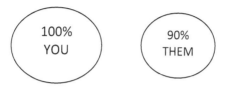

It's when the sneaky 10% shortage shows up that it starts to ignite a power struggle to get back the wholeness feeling. It's such a small drain we don't quite know why we are feeling off of our 100%. This is when we have to say to the other, "I love you and support you in your challenge." We should not fix or fill it with our energy.

Think about it like this: this is his challenge and if I love him, I will encourage and support him to fix it so he believes he can do it on his own. I will let him keep his crap and learn to fix it on his own, thus empowering him to become greater. Vice versa, you should expect the same behavior from him: not to come in and rescue you from your crap. Only loving encouragement is what builds an aligned relationship.

Until we find the strength to love ourselves unconditionally we probably have a hard to time giving love unconditionally to someone else without putting rules and restrictions on our love. But, no one can fill your needs and wants the way you can. This is why once we find enough love for ourselves to fill up to 100 %, we will not settle with allowing anyone drain us even just 1% because it feels so good to be in absolute joy, peace and *love*.

idi Tip: The first place to start healing yourself (no matter what the pain or symptoms are) is to implement a self-love. Every day, give something to yourself such as positive affirmations; starting with "I Love Myself" and "I deserve to be full of loving energy, thoughts and experiences."

PART III:
WORDS OF WARNING

9

ATTACHMENT

Train yourself to let go of everything you fear to lose
— Unknown

Usually one word says it all, and in this case it's

attachment. Attachment is an extra special word for me

because I used to be very attached to outcomes. Better

said, I was attached to rules (rules that I made up, by the

way). I was attached to what others thought of me,

attached to what I should know in order to be

considered smart, attached to appearance to be

considered attractive and healthy. Why was I so

attached to these things?

It's an easy answer. I wanted what I saw others around me doing and having. There is an understanding in our culture that living the "white picket fence" family life is right for all. You know, the life where dad works, mom raises kids, and we live in a safe neighborhood with all the kids becoming long–time friends. It must be right for me too, right? I thought so. I was attached to being the perfect image of a mother, having the perfectly clean and organized home, living the perfectly happy marriage with the perfectly peaceful family. I thought if I achieved this, then everyone would see me as successful.

Wow. That paragraph is hard for me to swallow. In no way do I resemble the person I used to be. I was so attached to what others' models of success looked like that I never asked myself if that was what I wanted. I never asked if those things brought me joy.

Inside I was dark, unhappy, heavy-hearted and uninspired. Some may wish for that perfect white picket fence life, but I did not. I started to see that the white picket fence life I had tried to create wasn't fulfilling my needs. It didn't seem to fit for me in today's world where divorce rates are through the roof, families everywhere are losing their homes, secure jobs with benefits and pensions are things of the past, and women and men are now playing in the same career arenas. The white picket fence life of the 1960s has shifted and the old rules don't seem apply. Why, might I ask, are we all so attached to proving we can make those unrealistic expectations happen?

Instead, how about proving to ourselves that we can create our own rules that are special for our families, careers, and lifestyles? If you create simplified rules, you have less to become attached to. The less attachment, the less pain and suffering you inflict on yourself.

Yes, you heard that right – on yourself. You created your own life – with your own rules to dictate if you perceive yourself a good or successful person. I know you do it. I did it. We all do it.

Do any of these sound familiar:

- If you get an F in school, you're dumb.
- If you lose a race, you're not athletic.
- If you don't get approval from your family on your marriage partner, you are cut off.
- If you don't talk like the group, you don't get to be part of our clique.

If the outcome doesn't happen, then we are losers. Well, if you are attached to the outcomes with rules, you will always be struggling to find peace. Is it better to be detached? Not necessarily. If we are detached we might find ourselves unengaged and missing life's experiences. We are human and meant to experience life in every way.

Try to live life in a non-attached form. Being non-attached is still experiencing but without concern for the result. When we flow through life without a need to find out the how the outcome will be, we can more easily accept things will work out. We should strive for that: a non-attachment life, without a pre-determined outcome. So if you don't like your life, it's time to look at who you are and what rules are in your life.

If you were to ask my daughters what guidelines we have in our home, they will first say, "There are no guidelines." Then they will correct themselves by saying, "Well, love, kindness, and compassion," which are essentially values and morals. This is what is so comical: they have no idea that by following those values, they will become them.

Whew. It's a big feat to become love, kindness and compassion, unless that's all you know. When someone is angry, disrespectful, dishonest, hurtful or just plain unaware of their actions towards them, my girls respond with love. They live by the quote "People need love most when they deserve it the least." (Unknown). It diffuses the experience much faster than responding with the same poor behavior. I have yet to see the day where a wrong corrects another wrong. So they aren't attached to the outcome since they live according to their love, kindness and compassion and not the how this will turn out.

Look at this: My six-year-old daughter worked very hard selling items for a school fundraiser. We parents all know the kids do it for the prizes they earn according to how many items they sell. Well, she had received three prizes for her efforts. When she returned to her cubby to retrieve her prizes, they were missing. When she told me who she thought may have taken them and what might have happened, I asked her to have kindness and compassion for the classmate she believed took them. I told her, "Never accuse another. Maybe he needed to feel what it was like to win a prize. That is more important. What goes around comes around. "

She didn't like what happened but she did understand: "If he did wrong, wrong would come back in some other way, right?" I agreed and told her that by sending compassionate understanding for the mishap, good will come back to her when she least expects it.

One day about a month later, she got into the car after school and said, "Mom, the boy who I thought took my prizes said sorry today and gave me this card he made." She then opened the envelope and was dazed by what he had put in it. Ten Dollars! To a six-year-old, that's called Rich Baby! And she was even more amazed by his letter inside, which read:

I am very sorry for taking your prizes, so here is two weeks of my allowance to purchase new ones. I am very sorry, please forgive me.

"Wow" is all I could come up with. I asked her, "Did you see how your love and compassion came back to you because you weren't attached to the outcome of how it would get fixed?" She said, "Yeah, $10 is way better than the prizes." My daughter allowed the experience of having something taken from her without being attached to it and it led her to receive something later that became even better than the original.

The lesson for me was this: If we need practice becoming something, start by teaching it to someone else. As I continue to try to teach my girls about love, kindness and compassion, I learn more myself.

idi Tip: Open yourself to living a non-attached lifestyle, so the outcomes can become greater than you wished for. Do this exercise: Review your life where you are currently experiencing discomfort. Then write down what the experience is on a piece of paper. Then burn the piece of paper. As the paper burns state, "I now accept the outcome that is for my highest good to appear." Then let it go from your thoughts.

10

3 MORE BACK AT YOU!

When you judge another, you do not define them, you define yourself. – Wayne Dyer

Take your hand and point your finger at the wall across from you. Now look at your hand. When you point at something else, there are three fingers pointing back at you.

Simply put, when you point fingers or accuse another of a thing, emotion, action, etc., it is a direct reflection of how you feel, but three times greater within. Yeah, it seems pretty simple but it's incredibly true!

Usually, when you find someone accusing another of being disrespectful and it's not true, it's easy to trace the three fingers back to the accuser as the guilty party. It's as if they have taken their insecurities and put them on a silver platter and handed them over to the other person.

The next time you find another person pointing a finger at you, let them! Allow them to express all their insecurities with pure silence on your end (except for a few "Uh huhs" from you so they know you are present). Then when they are finished, hand the silver platter back to them with compassion and let them keep it.

How do you hand it back? Well, just imagine a big silver platter with the word *disrespect* on it and say, "Here you go. This is your stuff, not mine. Now I gotta go!"

Well, maybe it's not a good idea to be that dramatic, but it thinking about it is a start. This will take some practice to do the right thing. Ask if they have proof that their accusation or statement is true. The likely answer would be a pause, then, "Um, No! But… "

This may be just their opinion and if they don't have proof, you need to let it go. You are confident in who you are! They are welcome to investigate internally. By looking within, they may begin to possibly understand why that topic distresses them to such a degree that they are trying to get rid of it and hand it over to you.

You should not be willing to keep the accusation for them. Internally understand and respect that is where they are without judging them as a bad, mean or disrespectful person.

It's difficult to do, I know. Here is a situation that arrived in my client Kelly's life. A very tall and muscular man accused her of being too masculine and aggressive.

Now in some ways I could argue his side, as her assertive, driven, confidant personality could be interpreted as masculine and aggressive to someone who is struggling with that specific trait. He may even find this type of personality intimidating to his inner fears of not being masculine and aggressive enough.

This man, on the exterior shell visually shows masculine and aggressive traits, but since he chose to accuse short, blond, sparkly, bling-wearing Kelly, his message was projecting very clearly.

Was she knocked off guard? At first, yes, as we all are when we get accused of a crime. We want to respond with, "Not Guilty!"

I agree that she is an assertive and confident woman with a strong personality. This is who she is and loves being just that. The finger pointed at her was in no way empowering and she chose to walk away without another word exchanged. Could she have snapped and gone the opposite way by attacking back? Absolutely. But instead, she appreciated him for who he was and realized that this may be something *he* might consider investigating on his own.

This is not easy to do. It has taken me so much practice to become calm and understanding when these lovely events happen. Over time when you do enough work within, it gets easier. You begin appreciating your own personal gifts and love each and every one of them fully. You love yourself for who YOU are so you do not get emotional or defensive about what others accuse you of.

If the descriptions were true, you would consider them compliments and empowering. If they are dis-empowering you would know that they are the accuser's own stuff in disguise. You would see they are just trying to hand them over to you as yours.

idi Tip: Louise L. Hay says it best: "If I want to be loved as I am, then I need to be willing to love others as they are." Send love to others when they are struggling or accusatory, but avoid sending back more accusations. Remember, accusations are a way people voice internal fear when they don't know another way. When you are being accused in the future, consider stepping away from it and standing present as the person you want to be with absolute strength, confidence and love.

11

TALKING TO A DOG

I know that you believe you understand what you think I said, but I'm not sure you realize that what you heard is not what I meant. — Robert McCloskey

"What are you talking about?" Have you heard that phrase said by another person, when all you can think is, "How could they have not heard me?" I am sure they heard you, but I would bet they did not understand you.

Communication is such a challenge for all of us when we think about it. We know what we are trying to convey in our heads, but often we find it hard to express that in words. Plus, sometimes there are no words to describe your thoughts and feelings. Now, don't get me wrong — I am a huge advocate for saying what you need to say, but

I am also a huge advocate for not being upset if another doesn't understand what you said.

If you were to have a conversation with a dog, you know you can say whatever you need to say and the dog will hear you. You are speaking a foreign language that has no meaning to the dog except that it's meaningful to you. You may get a few head tilts, grunts or a wagging tail in response, but the dog might not understand your language or tone. You have no expectation that the dog will have an opinion regarding what you said or is even going to start speaking back to you in verbal language.

Now here's the kicker: you don't hold the dog responsible for not responding properly. You have no delusion that the dog, out of the blue, will begin to use speech with perfect words to understand your dissertation. You give the dog acceptance that however it responds is perfect. You fully understand that the dog loves you and doesn't want to hurt you, just as you love the dog. You just needed to release what was inside, so you could get it out, and the dog listened.

You even love the dog after it had an accident on your new carpet and brought a messy bone into your bed. You forgave it after a little snuggle time and kisses, asking for forgiveness. You were completely comfortable with its mistakes and its inability to speak English back to you when you needed to talk.

Now let's consider this same scenario with regards to our partners, family, friends and kids. We love them, right? Is it unconditional? Do you expect them to understand you every time you have a conversation in your own personal language? Do you have the same love and forgiveness for them as you have for your dog? Is it possible for you to have more understanding for them?

This is a big communication mistake we humans make. We all think that if we speak words to another, they are understood. What we don't realize is that when we are speaking, the only one who understands our personal language is us. The message being conveyed is very likely coming out in a foreign language and ending in a misunderstanding. This is not an intentional misunderstanding on your end or the receiver's end. It's just simple misunderstanding.

We all speak differently yet we expect others to understand what we are saying immediately. Try something different: Consider that everyone you speak to from this point forward is hearing you in a foreign language. It's not that they don't want to hear your message; typically, they just don't understand it. They usually don't have answers and more importantly, they aren't supposed to. You have the answers *within,* remember? They, like the dog, should be considered just as a sounding board to get it out of you. You should not be expecting a response that you like.

If you can become clear that this is the case most of the time, you won't be so hurt each time they give you the "BEEEEP-WRONG ANSWER." When you're hurt, you get angry and send them to the dog house. Because you know you are looking outside yourself for answers from a foreigner, you can calm down, knowing the response or solution you receive in return may not match what you were hoping for. The times when it does, be grateful. Catalog that type of language to use with that person in future discussions.

Consider everyone you talk with has a dog's understanding, not computing much of what you said. So if you want to be heard, it is best to consider saying it in their language. Or, write it out on paper first to get your emotions out of the exchange. It will help you to be clearer on the specific message you are trying to convey.

idi Tip: In the next disagreement you have or conversation that isn't flowing, view the receiver as a dog, tilting its head, wondering what you are saying, and not intentionally wanting to offend or hurt your feelings. You can then walk away with less frustration and find internal understanding of what is really bothering you.

12

TRUTH

The starting point for improvement is to recognize the need.
— Masaaki Imai

Ready, set, go! *Tell the truth!* End of chapter!

Need I say more? OK, maybe a little.

Why is it we are so afraid of the truth? You have likely heard this before: "The truth will set you free." Pretty much, that's true. If you are speaking your personal truth, no matter how it may sound or what reaction it causes, it is true for you. It's easier to admit this than walking around making up more stories and other stories to explain those. And we've already visited what we do with stories.

This chapter is going to be short but I felt it was important to touch on it because truth comes up often with my clients. They withhold information as long as possible and then blaaaa, out of the blue, they say, "Well, I have to tell you the truth about something." Once they get it out, it's as if they are free from the bottled up tension they have been holding onto and then they begin to discuss the real topic that is bothering them.

Have you experienced this with friends, partners, kids, family? They tell you some of the story but then you ask enough questions and finally the truth comes out.

The simplest way to get to the truth is by being non-judgmental about their truth. Remember, it's *their* truth, not yours. So, just because they said or did something you don't approve of doesn't mean they need to be scolded for being a bad person. The best thing to do is to give them support and encouragement on how they can correct their struggle on their own. They are looking for someone to love them when they don't necessarily love themselves.

You have to be honest with yourself about a certain topic, and you can give yourself self-love. You may not think you deserve it if you are not happy with your actions, but nothing you do is bad or wrong. It was just a choice you made. It's a choice you can remake now to fit what you want to improve today. People need self-love and self-honesty.

Being honest with ourselves is more important than being honest with others. If you are honest with yourself, you won't have anything to hide or a need to be dishonest with others. It is an incredibly freeing and loving way to live.

Are you sometimes unsure of what to say, always trying to say what you think others want to hear and not ever feeling like you are really being you? That would be tough, unfulfilling, and a draining way to live. Maybe today is the day you decide that you have permission to live *your* truth. It is found inside of you and may take time to understand and develop. Recognizing your truth is more important than ignoring who you are and what you want. Trying to be what everyone else wants you to be is exhausting, and when you decide what you want and start being that, you'll see your self-confidence start to grow.

idi Tip: Pick one area of your work or home life where you are currently frustrated. Be honest with yourself on why it is really happening. What are you doing or avoiding? What have you previously been unaware of that would give you the tool to make it change? Think about it. Then tell yourself you are ready to make it better by making a change in yourself.

PART IV:
THE IDI SYSTEM

13

THE **idi** SYSTEM & HOW TO USE IT

The same amount of energy is required in order to aim high in life and to create abundance and prosperity as is required to accept drama, suffering and poverty. The difference between the two lies in your level of awareness.

This information, in many cases, could set you free from the constraints that keep you from realizing your greatest potential and free you to believe all of the good you deserve. Yet you cannot be free until you know exactly what shapes and directs your behavior and ultimately, what you want.

Everything I teach in **idi** consulting and personal development courses is based on the premise that thoughts are energy and they create things. Your thoughts create your life. For many people, old subconscious thoughts can be the foundation upon which their lives are created. Imagine a life created on only empowering thoughts.

Let me give you some background on how **idi** came to be. I have the most amazing, beautiful girls whom I thank God every day for blessing me with. I want to spend as much time as possible with them until they don't like me anymore and their friends are more exciting.

I wanted to be a stay-at-home mom, and I was determined to raise those kids one way or another. I knew in order to have what I wanted (to be with my kids and be a single parent), I would have to have a job that gave me flexibility. So I had started a new business that allowed me to make my own hours, take my kids to school, pick them up from school, bring them to work when necessary and be there they needed me.

I had walked out of my marriage and into a condo with no pictures on walls and barely any furniture, just a bed for the kids, a couch and kitchen table. The funny part is kids were jealous I didn't have a bed and asked how come I got to sleep on the floor. The girls wanted to sleep on the blow up mattress in my room instead of their own bed: "it's more fun and exciting, like camping," they said. What a contrast to my idea of the stability of a house with a white picket fence.

Now if getting divorced, moving to a place with no furniture, and starting a business (a salon by the way) weren't enough, I thought I could do hair and stand behind the chair and just "chit chat" about other people's problems when inspiration and teaching ran through my veins. That was much of the work I had done prior to my marriage ending, and my clients began to confide in me.

I began getting calls outside of the chair regarding our discussions during their hair service. I realized my time had reverted back to my coaching skills, but for free. That just wasn't gonna work.

I had founded Open Mind Consulting but closed it to pursue the world of beauty. Yet, as I was doing so, I pondered why I got a college degree in health and wellness, plus certifications in personal training and life coaching that I was just never going to fully use doing hair.

Hmmm...

Those phone calls pushed me to re-open Open Mind Consulting and run it in addition to the salon. Well, who would have known! I sure had no idea of the direction it would all take. Please tell me you're catching on to the scenario I was sitting in. Did it all overlap? Absolutely! I was building my skills to empower people from the inside out. But even greater, I was doing it foremost to get what I truly *wanted*! It was hard, confusing, draining and many times exhausting. But I was raising my girls. That was my want.

As my business grew, I knew I needed a general book for my clients to complete to assess what their wants were and I would know where to focus my coaching. **idi** started with "I Deserve It" dream workbooks that I created at home in my office with dollar store note pads and stickers.

Then as time passed, I had to step out of two businesses and focus on just one. Did I quit my day job? No! Please hear me, if one company that you love is not bringing you the income you need, do not quite your day job until the one you prefer is carrying you fully. So I proceeded to do hair part time and built **idi** to what it is today.

Now, let's explore how the **idi** system can be implemented into your life so you can create the life you want.

idi System

The **idi System** is designed as a tool to help you remember daily what you are worth and stop self-sabotage. We've made this drawing for you to understand each part. Hold your hand in the OK position to match the drawing.

- Pinkie finger means: Your purpose or **WAW (Why and What)**
- Ring finger means: **Ticking Clocks** that lead to self-sabotage or empowerment
- Middle finger means: **idi** – I Deserve It.
- Circle means: **The Big O** – What goes around comes around.

You can ask yourself daily, "Am I OK?"

WAW

WHY AND WHAT OR YOUR PURPOSE

Take the first step in faith. You don't have to see the whole staircase. Just take the first step. -Martin Luther King Jr.

Your pinky finger represents your purpose or **WAW**: **Why** you believe something would benefit your life right now and **What** will you get from it. This needs to be something bigger than you, something that is hard for you to comprehend but internally you know it's right. As simple as this sounds, it is difficult for many to answer, "WHAT do you want and WHY do you believe it?"

"I don't know" is the typical answer. Well, that's just a cop out. We know what we truly want in our lives deep down to our core. We need to acknowledge it and know that it may change through time. The Universe will not guide you to the right destination if it does not know what you want and why.

Know that it is different for everyone. If you already know it can be more specific things (like stay home with your kids, become a teacher, empower your team to success, travel to a new destination, start a new company, share your vision with others, write a book, etc.), follow it. I could never make a long enough list to create the wants for everyone, but you get the idea.

So that's the first part of the system. From now on ask yourself if you are on track with your WAW. Look at your the pinky finger and remember what you have stated as your personal WAW.

Ticking Clocks

We are what we repeatedly do. Excellence, then, is not an act, but a habit. — Aristotle

Let's talk about habits. According to the **Wikipedia** definition, habits *"are routines of behavior that are repeated regularly and tend to occur subconsciously. Habitual behavior often goes unnoticed in persons exhibiting it, because a person does not need to engage in self-analysis when undertaking routine tasks."*

We are conscious of the challenges we all face in life. However, we find it even more challenging to start new routines to make things better. We tend to be unaware of why we stumble to make changes or create better choices – because we may not be aware that the old habit needs replacement. Wow!

It sounds pretty complex, but we can think about it another way. Have you ever been around a clock or worn a watch that you could hear, "tick, tick, tick"? After some time has passed, you become oblivious to the ticking. You really need to pay attention to the clock in order to hear its ticking.

In the **idi System**, your ring finger represents "mental tics." Subconscious Clocks are your current mindsets, your ideas, and the little habits that your brain has developed over the years. The ticking clocks in our heads constantly remind us what programs our mental processes will run.

These tics, like dripping faucets, passing trains, or any other low volume noise, are drowned out of our attention. Unfortunately, we have learned to do that with thoughts as well. It's become our habitual pattern to play them over and over again in our heads, but like the clocks ticking we don't hear them. The clocks are there for most people, ticking negative messages, and some people have more than one ticking clock.

Sadly, there could be 10, 20 or even 50 years of constant ticking saying things like: "I'm not good enough," "I'm not lovable," "I am fat," "I am ugly," "I am unsuccessful," or "I am dumb." (The words are different for everyone but the occurrence is the same.) These thoughts are there, and they sit in our subconscious. We think they are drowned out of our attention, but they appear as roadblocks to our confidence and our drive. We think we can't do or have something because we have these inner messages that say we *can't*. (And remember how we feel about *can't*.) Habitual thinking leads to habitual behavior.

It would make sense then, that if you want to create less drama in your life and start getting new and healthier results, you've got to change your patterns or the clocks (thoughts) ticking in your head.

If your patterns are positive, you will have a happy, growth-oriented life, a healthy self-image, and the ability to adapt successfully to changes, upsets, and unforeseen events. Conversely, negative patterns can keep you imprisoned in old ways of thinking that can be very restricting.

You can see why it is an absolute necessity to pay attention to the thoughts that are ticking in our heads. It's also a necessity to change them if they are uninspiring in any way. This might be the greatest internal awareness you can make.

How and when do you change them? You have to first be conscious of the ticks that are taking place in your head, and prepare to change them when you start to feel "cuckoo." You must "take out its batteries" and reset it. Every day, sometimes even hourly, repeat positive messages to yourself. You can make a choice to replace the old ticking clocks, and start a new clock ticking with inspiring words.

Ask your friends to help you with words based on how they see you. It may take some time for it to become habitual and part of your subconscious thoughts. Keep in mind that it took time to create poor thoughts that became habitual, it won't take as long to employ new ones, but it will take some time for them to become habitual so they are ticking empowering messages even when you aren't paying attention.

Here is an exercise to get you started: Close your eyes and consider the last time you heard that inner voice talking in your head. Now listen for the disempowering words you may be using with yourself after a disagreement, missed goal, unachieved project, unfulfilled fitness or diet regime...you get it. Anything you find yourself not meeting your goal. Whatever that poor clock keeps saying, write it out on the next page.

Here are a few examples:
- I'm not good enough
- I'm not smart enough
- I'm not successful enough
- I'm not fit enough
- I'm not attractive enough
- I'm not loveable
- I'm NOT, I'm NOT, I'm NOT.

List the Disempowering Tics (Thoughts) ticking in your head:

Tic _____

Tic _____

Tic _____

Now, list the Empowering Tics (thoughts) you want ticking in your head. These are new words to trump those disempowering ones that have been ticking subconsciously. These are empowering words that will encourage you from now on each time you hear a poor clock start up.

Example: I am Amazing, Deserving, Strong, Successful

Tic _____

Tic _____

Tic _____

Knowing what you want to change is half the effort of changing them. Remember some of us have had a habitual tic taking place for many years, so it may take time to change. This is a daily habit you will need to commit to in order to see its effects on your life. The effort is worth it, because these ticking thoughts will stop or encourage you to get what you want, and you have the power to make them encouraging.

Occasionally, we all hear clock tics in our heads that randomly get loud and say, "you are nuts and you are not doing it right." Or, "you are not deserving of love, success, friends, or fun if you continue to act like this." Oh, how the clocks can tic, tic, tic until you get quiet and see the new things you have built in your life. Then you can realize, "I do deserve this!" and proceed to take out the self-defeating clock's batteries to silence them and begin hanging new clocks in your head.

Get your empowering thoughts/tics in order like, "I deserve to be with my kids, to have healthy relationships, friends, fun and joy." I finally began to believe in my soul and say to myself "I love myself in every way," no matter what is happening outside of me.

You'll need to rewind or reset your good clocks from time to time because they take a while to become unconscious, continuous, habitual sounds.

I Deserve It

The minute you settle for less than you deserve, you get even less than you settled for. — Maureen Dowd

The third finger represents our company name, I Deserve It. As you know from earlier chapters, my "want" of staying with my kids created **idi**, but as I've grown and matured, my want has changed. Now, it's to raise the self-worth of the people on this planet; to empower others to know that they are deserving of love, success, joy, prosperity and fun.

I see it when I'm watching:

- A runner push through the end of a marathon with a hat says "**idi**"
- A woman embrace her femininity because her WAW is to have and care for a baby
- An executive developing an empowered organization to create a breakthrough gadget because his WAW is to change the world
- A client whose WAW is to be in a loving relationship.

These are joyous things to witness because the people I touched have started to understand that our power stems from our self-worth or our perception of what we deserve. We need to identify our own power and learn to use that power.

How can you do that? The key principle here is Believe and Deserve:

How do you teach little kids to remember which direction the b's and d's face when they are learning to write? You show them that b comes before d with your hands like this:

b  d

Hold your left hand up and form the letter *b* now hold your right hand up and form the letter *d*. Similarly, *Believing* comes before *Deserving*, and you can think of this when you look at your hands.

This is an example of habitual learning: You see it enough on your fingers and it will just become part of your memory.

So, time for more exercises. Let me ask you a question about the letter d? What is one thing you want?

Answer: _____

Do you have it? If not, then you probably don't believe you deserve it. Very simply, we all have what we believe we deserve: Poor relationships, no money, struggling businesses, inability to conceive, lack of friends, no time – you get the picture. But on the positive side, we all have the inner power to feel and experience what we habitually re-program ourselves to think we deserve, like: good health, enough food, or strong faith, because there is enough food, money, shelter, health and love on this planet for everyone to have an abundance of each – and we would still have a surplus!

But for so many it seems one or several of these things are unattainable. Why is it so easy for one person to achieve financial abundance but struggle with health, then another with the good health, struggles to find food? This topic perplexed me for years.

Here's a great example: As I taught this system to a client, she expressed to me the desire to create a more abundant and prosperous company. She felt stuck. She was a realtor and given our current economy she felt she was not able to expand her business. She didn't feel deserving of more.

At that time, she was on a detour from her path and unfamiliar with the surroundings. She was lost as to which direction to turn to get back on her true path, and then I reminded her of these three words: "You Deserve It."

She had to create a WAW bigger than she was, so she chose to create her WAW. She would expand her network to represent or show homes in any price range no matter how grand it was. She realized that a contract for a $100,000 home and $1,000,000 home were the same. She also said that each client was the same, with individual needs that she had the ability to serve. Once she opened up her WAW to all areas of the arena she was working in, her business began to grow, even in this tough real estate market.

The **idi** system helped her interrupt her self-sabotage based on what the world outside was telling her wasn't possible and allowed her to create the business of her dreams.

Only when we create a WAW that we believe in do we dedicate ourselves to the necessary actions to create it in our lives. When you start believing on the inside what you are worthy and capable of, then you will feel you deserve it.

Is it as scary as a horror film? Sometimes it could be, but it's worth it for you to see your true power within. It is never as scary as your imagination created it to be. I know because I have lived it.

Now It's Your Turn!

The Big "O"

All that we are is the result of what we have thought.
— Buddha

Look at your index finger and thumb making the shape of a circle, symbolizing the circle of life. You may have heard me reference this in other chapters: "What goes around, comes around." I am a firm believer because I have seen it over and over again. We may not always see the fruits of our thoughts, efforts, actions or kindnesses immediately, but when the time is right, they will come back to us.

The world returns to you a reflection of who you are inside. Said another way, the Universe gives back to you the same amazing things you believe within. It sees the work you have done on yourself to become stronger, healthier, empowered, inspiring, and loving. When you build a better life that inspires others to do the same, goodness will be sent back to you in a greater fashion than you ever expected, and when you least expect it.

The *idi* System Recap

In training the mind, perspective is of crucial importance. We cannot expect to transform our minds in a few minutes or even a few weeks, thinking, perhaps, that the blessings of an enlightened individual will enable us to obtain immediate results. Such an attitude is not realistic. It takes a long time, sometimes years or even decades; but if we persevere, there is no doubt we will make progress. – Dalai Lama

The **idi** system was created to help you get out of your own way and get on your way to your personal WAW. To get the biggest benefit, you must practice it. Here's a recap of the System to help you.

The Four Parts of the idi System:

1. WAW
2. Check Your Tics
3. idi
4. The Big O

PARTING THOUGHTS: THE *DRAMA DETOX* PRESCRIPTION

It always seems impossible, until it's done. — Nelson Mandela

The research shows placebos work in many cases. Why? Because we believe! We are told something is supposed to calm us down, then we allow our bodies to adjust to that state of mind because we are taking a magic pill.

When physicians use placebos, the patients have no idea if it is a sugar pill or real medication, but they are told it is real, and they believe it will make us better. What they believe often happens. Hmmm, this got me thinking about creating thoughts in our heads (that we are healthy, strong, fit, successful, beautiful, loveable, loving, kind, and balanced). If we say them enough times, will we believe it? Yes! Now, it does take more than happy thoughts, but empowering specific thoughts can start the process in motion.

Here's an example: If you want to create wealth in your life, think about how that would be. What would be the same, what would be different? Then, behave as though you have your wish. Make paper money with eight or more zeros on it and put it in your wallet, money clip, in your car, on your mirror, computer screen, everywhere. The fake money is like a placebo. You keep telling yourself, "This is my income." When it is all you see, you start to believe it is what you are capable of. Your brain at that point begins to question how your life really is and you begin to start making choices you wouldn't normally make that would support you bringing in income. The Universe begins adjusting your life. You might see this in guiding you to become more marketable if you own your own company, falling into a better job, or finding additional sources of income in ways you weren't expecting.

Naturally, you begin to heal and make adjustments to allow it to become real. If your goal is hugely skewed from your current lifestyle, it may take a little longer, but I truly believe everything is possible. You need to simply allow the energy to be built up to its fullest potential to create it.

So imagine your doctor told you that you must repeat eight things to yourself daily or you will get very ill. Would you do it? Let's try an exercise. How about if Dr. Daune prescribed a Self-Talk Prescription in the form of a few affirmations to take in and repeat daily or even hourly.

This prescription is easiest to relate to if you understand its origin. Think back in time to when you were young. Think back to a favorite meal that you enjoyed growing up. You remember it from the smell in the house, the person making it (mom, dad, grandparent). Each time you enjoyed that meal, candy, food or drink, it triggered happy thoughts. That sensory experience still will trigger the same emotional response when you eat it.

I *love* carrot cake. Until I began teaching this sensory recall patterning, I never realized why I had such joy when I ate it. When I was a little girl, I would make it from scratch with my grandmother, from shredding fresh carrots to whipping the cream from the carton to make frosting. I have such happy emotions wrapped around carrot cake.

Do you see where this prescription we are going to make is geared to? You are trying to trigger an emotional response from some of your strongest senses, taste and smell. When you do this next exercise, choose a small trigger that will stimulate your empowering thoughts like my carrot cake trigger. Find a bottle (any size), fill it with your favorite nut, bite-size candy (like cinnamon hearts, licorice bites, or M&Ms) or any treat. Then write down, on the bottle itself or on a label, the self-talk prescription set below. Each time you need a pick-me-up, eat a piece and read the affirmation on the bottle. This should become a daily dose of empowerment. Some days, you may need to eat half the bottle; go ahead and overdose on these affirmations.

Choose the ones that inspire you:

- *I love myself and all my gifts.*
- *I love my healthy, fit strong body.*
- *I am successful today.*
- *I am abundant in every way and I welcome all prosperity into my life.*
- *I am a magnet to financial prosperity.*
- *I deserve to live the life that is perfect for me.*
- *I am love and I am loveable and welcome loving healthy relationships in my life.*

Feel free to add more – you can't overdose on these affirmations. These are just suggestions to get the ball rolling.

This is the part I love the most: even if you don't believe, *do it anyway*. There is a phrase, "Fake it till you make it." Even if it takes longer than you wish, keep up the placebo. I am telling you, you will begin to believe. It will become very potent and healing if you give it the time to work. The **idi** System check should be your daily prescription to fill your subconscious with your new empowering beliefs. This prescription is your personally-designed prescription to detox your internal life so your external world reflects it.

Start Today:

1. Set your personal **idi** check as a daily exercise.

    To confirm if you're OK, check your fingers.

2. Fill your personal affirmation bottle today as your daily reminder to engage your senses into your purpose.
3. Teach another person how to do the same to engage another in your WAW.

I believe you deserve to see all your wishes come true. Go get it – You Deserve It!

Remember the 12 **idi Tips** from each chapter:

1. **idi Tip**: Start detoxing your life (stew) today. The most important step in getting rid of drama is personal awareness. The fastest way to clean our own house is becoming aware that it needs to be cleaned. Often we are just used to situations, so we miss the need to clean. What areas of your life could use a cleanse? Think about it. What areas would you be able to label it as having drama in them? Start to evaluate them.

2. **idi Tip**: When the drama in your life is boiling, get a piece of paper out and draw a circle on it. Then write all the ingredients currently in your life, good and bad. Put a big X on the outside of the circle (representing you and your outside perspective). Choose to see all these ingredients as individuals, things, and experiences. As the X on the outside, you can begin to address each ingredient inside the circle, one at a time. Then

you can take out the bitter, unhealthy ingredients until you have a simpler stew, one that you could enjoy. When you put it on paper, you take it out of your head, which relieves you of that mental drama.

3. **idi Tip**: Can you think of one thing you would like to turn from frustration and bitterness into contentment? One thing, one person, one situation, or just one plaguing thought that if you changed your ways, the situation would change too. Be honest with yourself. You don't have to explain it to others; you just have to explain it to yourself to make your insides happy. Acknowledging it is all it takes to start making it reality. It may take some time, though, so remember patience.

4. **idi Tip**: This was a long chapter, given that relationships are a potent part of our lives and help build our character. When evaluating relationships, use this simple scale: if it makes

you cry, it might be time to say goodbye. If it makes you smile, do what it takes to keep it.

5. **idi Tip:** What story do you tell yourself that has *can't* in it? Give yourself permission to live in the truth of now and create a new story with "I can" today.

6. **idi Tip**: Find a notebook, poster board, sticky notes, anything you can start documenting your grandest Dreams today. Make a list, draw pictures or cut and paste. Start now. Make big wishes and show the Universal Genie what you want!

7. **idi Tip**: See if you can make a list of 100 qualities – spiritual, emotional, physical, and moral. This is a personal wish list so don't question your wants. Just know some will be adaptable when the right fish with blue, yellow and turquoise shows up.

8. **idi Tip**: The first place to start healing yourself (no matter what the pain or symptoms are) is to

implement a self–love. Every day, give something to yourself such as positive affirmations; starting with "I Love Myself" and "I deserve to be full of loving energy, thoughts and experiences."

9. **idi Tip**: Open yourself to living a non-attached lifestyle, so the outcomes can become greater than you wished for. Do this exercise: Review your life where you are currently experiencing discomfort. Then write down what the experience is on a piece of paper. Then burn the piece of paper. As the paper burns state "I now accept the outcome that is for my highest good to appear." Then let it go from your thoughts.

10. **idi Tip**: Louise L. Hay says it best: "If I want to be loved as I am, then I need to be willing to love others as they are." Send love to others when they are struggling or accusatory, but avoid sending back more accusations. Remember, accusations are a way people voice internal fear when they don't know another way. When you

are being accused in the future, consider stepping away from it and standing present as the person you want to be with absolute strength, confidence and love.

11. **idi Tip**: In the next disagreement you have or conversation that isn't flowing, view the receiver as a dog, tilting its head, wondering what you are saying, and not intentionally wanting to offend or hurt your feelings. You can then walk away with less frustration and find internal understanding of what is really bothering you.

12. **idi Tip**: Pick one area of your work or home life where you are currently frustrated. Now be honest with yourself on why it is really happening. What are you doing or avoiding? What have you previously been unaware of that would give you the tool to make it change? Think about it. Then tell yourself you are ready to make it better by making a change in yourself. Pick one area of your work or home life where you are

currently frustrated. Be honest with yourself on why it is really happening. What are you doing or avoiding? What have you previously been unaware of that would give you the tool to make it change? Think about it. Then tell yourself you are ready to make it better by making a change in yourself.

You can start with your daily **idi** checks and begin to live today the life *you want*. Begin the life that inspires others to see you as the inspiration that you truly are. We all have gifts – it's up to you to see them within and sharing them with others.

JOURNAL SPOT

This journal section is provided to capture your ah-ha! moments. There is no right or wrong way to use this section. Just keep all of your new positive, motivational, inspiring guidance here. This section can be whatever you make it, but remember, no rules. A grocery list, an affirmation that sings to you, a reminder to get dry cleaning or just a place to express yourself.

JOURNAL SPOT

JOURNAL SPOT

JOURNAL SPOT

ABOUT THE AUTHOR

Daune Thompson

Daune has earned a Bachelor of Science degree in Kinesiology from University of Wisconsin-Milwaukee and is a Certified Life Coach. She has developed customized training programs and employee-relations courses for Fortune 500 companies such as Kimberly-Clark Corporation and Menasha Corporation and has held the position as Director of Training and Development for a national training company and speaker's bureau.

Her experience extends to management in the health and wellness, self-help and nutrition industries. Daune has an extensive fitness background and has taught at the University of Wisconsin-Milwaukee and Dow Chemical. This unique expertise provides her the strong foundation needed to be an effective and results-driven life coach and personal mentor.

She has authored self-empowerment workbooks for both adults and children entitled: *I Deserve It – A Supportive Guide to Creating And Living The Life Of Your Dreams.*

Daune is passionate, inspiring and engaging in her ability to inspire people to overcome their challenges and fears, leading them to create a more effective and successful business or personal life. You will be motivated by her energetic, empowering and supportive guidance.

ACKNOWLEDGEMENTS

Completing this book has been such a journey for me. It has been simmering in me for years, and I am finally able to make it a reality with the help of wonderful people in my life.

I want to especially thank my mother, Dedra, for her continued support and encouragement to share my work with the world. She is such an inspiration and I am blessed to follow in her footsteps.

Thank you to my beautiful girls for trusting in their mommy's "silly" (as they say) techniques intended to empower them as our future leaders. They inspire me every day to become stronger. Also, thanks to all the incredible friends in my life who have continually used my tools to better their lives – if only to prove to *me,* when I questioned myself, that they work.

Thank you to my brother Lance Jaze, for designing the cover and graphics of this book. Your artistic ability is brilliant and I am blessed to have your talents shown in my work.

I must step forward and acknowledge all of my amazing clients. They have pushed me to put my spoken words into print: I have finally done so, empowered by their constant gratitude for my presence in their lives.

Now for Bonnie, you have such incredible patience, understanding and insight in the editing process (about which I was shaking in my boots). I truly could not have done this project without you. Thank you from my soul for your "kid gloves" support in pushing me to make this dream come true.

So this is a formal thank you to all of you who have inspired me to want to fulfill your wishes. In doing so, I fulfill my own.

RESOURCE DIRECTORY

idi Personal Success Coaching

This empowering coaching package will help you find the truth about who you are what you want. It will bring awareness that will ignite your passion and set you on an unstoppable path to success. Take control of your destiny and discover your purpose in life. Discover the freedom to live the life *you* want. Become more confident & assertive. Boost your self-esteem with full life balance. More info: www.ideserveitnow.com

idi Group/Team Success Coaching

How you react to relationships with others, whether it's your *business partners, personal partners, parents, siblings or children* can reveal deep truths about your true capacity for success in all areas. All work & no play makes for imbalance but **idi** has created a coaching system for achievement in both.

Men's Master Mind Boot Camp

CEOs, Owners, Presidents, Senior Executives: This is for you!
Professional Presence – Business Master Mind Design: Get clarity, direction & accountability with your Power Team. **Partnerships** – Create partnerships that support instead of drain you. **Social Presence** –Men's Social/Play Outings (Golf, Entertainment, Down Time). **Personal Self** – Eradicate old, limiting beliefs that keep you playing small in every way, plus Personal Image Design. All work & no play makes for imbalance, but **idi** has created a boot camp with both.

Self-Mastery Boot Camp

Strengthen your integrity by having your actions on the outside world line up with what you value on the inside. It's time to redirect your thoughts from an environment that has been a factor defining who you are, how you feel, or how you live. You will leave these **idi** courses with tools that will hold you accountable to SUCCESS. For Monthly Meetings listings, visit: *http://www. meetup. com/idi-I-Deserve-It-Self-Mastery-Boot-Camp/*

idi Membership

The All-Access pass to **idi** Membership includes: 1 Year "Ask Daune" access * **idi** affirmation picture pages updated monthly (keychain sold separately) * **idi** Mobile App * Access to additional coaching pages * Monthly News Updates * *http://www. Ideserveitnow. com/Create-an-account.html*

idi – I Deserve It Tools

I Deserve It –Hats, shirts, bracelets, books, sticky notes, key chains and more to keep you habitually reminded daily of what you deserve. Visit: *www. ideserveitnow.com/products*

idi Mobile App

We are excited to share our NEW Mobile App for your PHONE. Empower yourself daily with Affirmations & Encouragement. Scan this tag with your phone or this link address: *http://fantagz. com/ideserveit.aspx#home*

MASTER YOURSELF
AND YOUR WORLD BECOMES A MASTERPIECE

WWW.IDESERVEITNOW.COM

INFO@IDESERVEITNOW.COM

SCOTTSDALE, AZ 85258

DAUNE THOMPSON

480. 703. 2019

Your Daily idi Reminders

	### *idi –Black Leather Bracelet* Small – Adjustable to fit women's or children's wrists
	### *idi –Sterling Cuff* Small, Medium, and Large sizes available for women and men
	### *idi –Keychain* Your Vision is never out of sight.
	### *idi – Adult Dream Book* This empowering dream book is designed for you to create a powerful reminder of who you are and everything you Deserve in this life.
	### *idi – Kids' Dream Book* This dream book is for kids to create positive pictures and affirmations of who they are and everything they wish for in their life.

173

	idi Hats **idi – do you?**
	**idi Shirts** **idi – do you?**
	Personal/Corporate **Success Coaching**
All items can be purchased at **www. ideserveitnow. com**	

Made in the USA
Lexington, KY
15 December 2014